Jenni Vive

Jenni Vive

Unforgettable, Baby!

A Life in Pictures
Su vida en fotos

Edited by the Jenni Rivera Estate

ATRIA PAPERBACK

New York   London   Toronto   Sydney   New Delhi

ATRIA PAPERBACK
An Imprint of Simon & Schuster, Inc.
1230 Avenue of the Americas
New York, NY 10020

First Atria Paperback edition October 2015

ATRIA PAPERBACK and colophon are trademarks of Simon & Schuster, Inc.

For information about special discounts for bulk purchases, please contact Simon & Schuster Special Sales at 1-866-506-1949 or business@simonandschuster.com.

The Simon & Schuster Speakers Bureau can bring authors to your live event. For more information or to book an event, contact the Simon & Schuster Speakers Bureau at 1-866-248-3049 or visit our website at www.simonspeakers.com.

Interior design by Julian Peploe

Manufactured in the United States of America

10 9 8 7 6 5 4 3 2 1

Library of Congress Cataloging-in-Publication Data

Rivera, Jenni.
    Jenni vive / Jenni Rivera.—First Atria paperback edition.
      pages cm
    1. Rivera, Jenni. 2. Rivera, Jenni—Portraits. 3. Singers—Biography.
ML420.R653 A3   2015
782.42164092 B   2015014659

ISBN 978-1-5011-0131-1
ISBN 978-1-5011-0132-8 (ebook)

I'd like to sing a couple songs for you that are very special to me. The first one, which I wrote myself, is about my own life and the wonders that God has been able to work through it. I've always compared my life to a butterfly's metamorphosis. My life hasn't been easy at all; it's been very difficult at times. I could compare it to a caterpillar's existence: it crawls along the ground, suffering; it's not at all pretty, and all kinds of things happen to it. But God is so great, that thanks to a metamorphosis, that caterpillar becomes a butterfly and takes flight, free, with all of its colors. And that's the way I feel today.

—*Jenni Rivera, speaking at the Nokia Theatre in 2010 before launching into the song "Mariposa de Barrio (Neighborhood Butterfly)"*

Quiero, si me lo permiten, cantarles un par de canciones muy especiales para mí. Una la compuse yo, hablando de mi propia vida y de las maravillas que ha hecho Dios con ella. Siempre he comparado mi vida con la metamorfosis de una mariposa. Mi vida no ha sido nada fácil; ha sido muy difícil. Podría yo comparar mi vida a la de una oruga que se arrastra por los suelos, y que sufre mucho, y que no es bonita, y a la que le pasan y le suceden muchas cosas. Pero Dios es tan grande que, a través de la meta-morfosis, esa oruga se convierte en una mariposa, y llega a volar libre, con todos sus colores. Como yo lo estoy haciendo hoy.

—*Jenni Rivera, antes de cantar "Mariposa de Barrio" en un concierto en el teatro Nokia en 2010*

Contents—
Contenido

Letter from Jenni's Mother

My dearest daughter,

When we arrived in California, I learned I was pregnant. I knew it wasn't the ideal time, because we had only recently arrived to the United States and we were very poor. But God in his wisdom felt it was the right time for you to come into my life. I happily carried you in my womb when I understood that it was God's will. I spent those nine happy months eating lots of tomatoes and drinking tomato juice with fresh lemons. Until this day, whenever I see a tomato I think of you, my love. The day you were born, I remember having labor pains all day long. Your dad had never seen me in that kind of pain during labor and he was really worried about me. The moment you were born and they told me you were a girl, I cried tears of joy and immediately regretted not being excited the very first moment I learned I was pregnant. Later, when your dad came into the room, I told him, "Look! It's a beautiful baby girl, wrapped in a little blanket!" He was overjoyed. He so wanted a little girl! Your dad and I were thrilled with the little queen who sat on the throne in our hearts. Years later came Rosie, your own little doll, with whom you happily shared your place of honor.

As time passed, everyone loved spoiling you: your daddy, your brothers, and I. Your brothers made you into a rough-and-tumble little girl, but they were always caring and careful with you. You were a fighter, sure, but you were smart, too. We never had trouble with your grades in school. You were always an intelligent and loving daughter.

You left me too early. You married very young, but you gave me the sweetest grandchildren in the world. Chiquis was my first grand-child and I felt very motherly toward her. I remember you telling me, "*I'm* her mother!" Then came sweet Jacqie and my beautiful boy, Michael, whom we called Tonguito. After that, Jenicka and Johnny Angel. Five beautiful souls who filled my life with love and who still fill me with vitality when I see you through them.

You know what I'll always remember? The way you supported me in everything, with your love, with your warm embrace, with your unconditional support in even the most difficult times. Anything I ever needed, you were always right there. I thank God for your life, for having brought me so much love, caring, and respect.

You know, when I traveled with you during the Mexico tour in November 2012, I came along even though I felt bad after having that fall. But I didn't quit! I remember you asked me, "Mom, do you want me to buy you a ticket so you can fly home early or do you want to fly back with me?" And I said, "I'll go back the day you do." I always wanted to be by your side and enjoy you as much as I could. We enjoyed that tour with your cousins Edith and Laura because you always shared your blessings with the rest of us.

Time passed, and on December 6 you asked me, "Mom, will you come with me to Monterrey?" and I told you, "No, because I'd rather be at the finals of *La Voz Mexico*. I want to be there when you win—and you *are* going to win." And you told me, "I have really good singers, right?" You always did. By this point, I assume you know you won. You won then and you'll keep on winning. As always, you invited several people to go along to Monterrey, but God called only you on that occasion.

God has our days numbered. And on December 9, 2012, you lived your last day on earth here with us before God called you to be by His side . . . to live in a new home, in a world very different from the one you came from; to walk along streets paved in gold and oceans of crystal blue to praise the Lord as you always did. Because that was always your mission: to sing to the Lord. I know you are at His side and at peace; there's no doubt in my mind about that. You don't have to cry anymore and your knee doesn't hurt like it used to. We will see each other again one day, and we will hug and sing to a God that never left our side, the king of kings, the lord of lords. We will adore him together, you, me, your brothers, and your sister.

Thank you, *hija*, for all your love and support, for having blessed me with your children and surrounded me with loved ones who call me *mother*. I miss you terribly, but you bequeathed me an inheritance of love that will last me until we meet again.

You sowed so much love in this world, and you must be able to see how your fans, your true admirers, returned that love to me. They care for me and pamper me, thanks to the love you showed them.

I'm sending you all my love, my hugs and kisses, and we will continue to bring glory to God and to await the day that He calls us to His side so we can be together again, forever. I love you very much. Your brothers and sister miss you as well. They await the moment of our reunion, and I yearn to hear you laugh together once again.

Your mother who loves you,
Rosa Rivera

Carta de la madre de Jenni

Querida hija,

Cuando llegamos a California, descubrí que estaba embarazada. Supe que no era el tiempo indicado, porque estábamos recién llegados a los Estados Unidos y éramos muy pobres. Pero a Dios le pareció que era el tiempo correcto para que llegaras a mi vida. Te llevé en mi vientre con alegría después de que comprendí que este era el designio de Dios. Viví los nueve meses de mi embarazo feliz, comiendo muchos tomates y jugo de tomate con limón. Hasta el día de hoy, cada vez que veo tomates pienso en ti, mi niña. El día en que tú naciste, recuerdo que estuve con dolores de parto todo el día. Tu papá nunca me había visto en esos momentos dolorosos de parto y se preocupó mucho por mí. Cuando llegó el momento en que naciste y me dijeron que eras una niña, lloré lágrimas de felicidad y me arrepentí de no haberte deseado al principio. Luego, cuando tu papá entró al cuarto, le dije: "¡Mira! Es una niña blanca peloncita envuelta en una cobijita". Él estaba muy feliz. ¡Tenía tantas ganas de tener una niña! Tu papá y yo nos pusimos muy felices con nuestra reina que reclamó su trono en nuestros corazones. Años después, llegó Rosie, tu muñeca, con quien compartiste con gusto tu lugar.

Pasó el tiempo y eras una niña chiqueada y mimada por todos: tu papi, tus hermanos y yo. Tus hermanos te hicieron una niña peleonera y fuerte, pero siempre cuidada y custodiada por ellos. Eras peleonera sí, pero muy inteligente. Nunca hubo problemas por tus calificaciones en la escuela. Siempre fuiste una hija inteligente y cariñosa.

Te me fuiste muy pronto. Te casaste joven, pero me diste los nietos más cariñosos del mundo. Chiquis fue mi primera nieta, y me sentía mamá de ella. Recuerdo que me decías, "¡Yo soy su mamá!" Luego, llegó la dulce Jacqie y mi niño hermoso, a quien le decía mi Tonguito, Michael. Después, Jenicka y Johnny Ángel. Cinco alegrías que llenaron mi vida de amor al nacer, y aún llenan mi vida al verte a través de ellos.

¿Sabes qué? Recuerdo siempre cómo me apoyaste en todo, con tu cariño, con tus abrazos y tu apoyo incondicional en momentos difíciles. Con todo lo que necesitara, allí estabas y estarás siempre. Vivo agradecida de Dios por tu vida y por haberme llenado de tanto amor, cariño y respeto.

Sabes, cuando anduvimos juntas en la gira de México en noviembre de 2012, te acompañé aunque me sentía mal porque me había caído, ¡pero no me rajé! Recuerdo que me preguntaste, "Mamá, ¿se devuelve conmigo o le saco el boleto antes?", y te contesté, "Me devuelvo el día que tú te devuelvas". Siempre quise estar a tu lado, y disfrutar contigo lo más que pude. Gozamos de esa gira junto a tus primas Edith y Laura, porque siempre compartiste tus bendiciones con todos.

El tiempo pasó, y el día 6 de diciembre me preguntaste, "Mamá, ¿vas conmigo a Monterrey?", y te dije, "No, porque quiero ir a la final de *La Voz México*. Quiero verte ganar, porque tú vas a ganar". Me dijiste, "Sí. ¿Verdad, mamá, que tengo buenos cantantes?" Sí, la mejor tenía a los mejores. ¿Me imagino que ya sabes que ganaste? Ganaste y sigues ganando. Como siempre, invitaste a varios a Monterrey, pero Dios solo tenía el llamado a ti en esa ocasión.

Dios tiene nuestros días contados. El 9 de diciembre de 2012, cumpliste tu tiempo aquí con nosotros, y Dios te llevó a cumplir tu deber junto a Él . . . A vivir en una casa nueva, en un mundo muy diferente al que tenías; a caminar por las calles de oro y el mar de cristal y alabar por siempre a nuestro Señor. Porque esa era tu misión: cantarle al Señor. Sé que estás junto a Él y estás en paz, de eso no me cabe duda. Ya no lloras y no te duele la rodilla. Allá nos encontraremos, nos abrazaremos y juntas le cantaremos a un Dios que nunca nos ha dejado, al Rey de Reyes y Señor de Señores. Lo adoraremos juntos, tus hermanos, tu hermana y yo.

Gracias, hija, por todo el cariño, el amor y por haberme bendecido con tus hijos y rodeado con tanta gente que me dice *madre*. Me haces mucha falta, pero me dejaste una herencia de amor que me sostendrá hasta que te vea otra vez.

Sé que sembraste mucho amor y verás cómo me dan amor tus seguidores, que han sido verdaderos admiradores. Me cuidan y me miman gracias al amor que tú les diste.

Mi hija, te mando muchos besos y abrazos, y seguiremos glorificando a Dios y esperando ese día que Él nos llame a Su presencia y nos junte para siempre. Te quiero mucho. Tus hermanos y hermana te extrañan también. Esperan ese momento con ansias, y yo anhelo escucharlos reír juntos otra vez.

Tu madre que te quiere,
Rosa Rivera

Jenni's Heart—
El corazón de Jenni

2

Childhood—Niñez

Ten years old: Long Beach, California

A los diez años: Long Beach, California

@jennirivera 28 Nov 2012

"At King's Park in the LBC . . . that's where you'll find me. Hangin with my homies and my friends" . . . Summertime in the LBC.

If I had the opportunity to speak to a young immigrant girl who just arrived to the US, the advice I would have for her would be: ask, speak, and search; because there are opportunities here. And remember that you aren't the only immigrant, nor the last to come to this country. Many that have come before you have succeeded. It is possible!

—Jenni Rivera

Si tuviera la oportunidad de hablar con una joven inmigrante recién llegada a los Estados Unidos, mi primer consejo sería: pregunta, habla y busca. Sí hay oportunidades aquí. Recuerda que no eres ni la única ni la última inmigrante que viene a este país. Muchos han llegado antes que tú y han tenido éxito. ¡Sí se puede!

—Jenni Rivera

Siblings
(Hermanos):
Gustavo, Lupe,
Pedro, mamá
Rosa, and Janney

Siempre fui la patita fea entre mis amigas.
—Jenni Rivera

Among my friends, I was always the ugly duckling.
—Jenni Rivera

Left to right (De izquierda a derecha): **Janney, mamá Rosa, Juan, Gus, Pete, and Lupe**

Out here it's like I'm someone else . . . Won't take nothing but a memory from the house that built me.

—"The House That Built Me" by Miranda Lambert

Es mi orgullo haber nacido en el barrio más humilde.

—"El hijo del pueblo" de José Alfredo Jiménez

Janney at twelve years old

Janney a los doce años

9

Family Life —
La vida en familia

Donde esté tu tesoro,
allí estará también tu
corazón.

—Mateo 6:21

For where your treasure is, there
your heart will be also.

—Matthew 6:21

TELEMUNDO
you're on
CASINO · HOTEL
LAS VEGAS, NV
LAS VEGAS
TELEMUNDO

Don Pedro, Jenni, doña Rosa

Ya no vivo entre tanta pobreza, vivo como mi padre soñó. No ambiciono tampoco riqueza, la sangre de indio es mejor.

—"Sangre de Indio" de José Arturo Rodríguez González

Doña Rosa and Jenni

Fuiste tú la fiel y confiable amiga, la que ha marcado mi vida, fuiste tú. Fuiste tú el ser que me ha consolado, que aún no deja mi lado, fuiste tú.

—"Homenaje a mi madre" de Jenni Rivera

Jenni, Esteban, and Minister Pedro
Rivera, Jr., September 8, 2010.
Brother, pastor, and, on her wedding
day, her minister.
*Jenni, Esteban y el ministro Pedro
Rivera, Jr., el 8 de septiembre de 2010.
Hermano, pastor y, el día de su
boda, su ministro.*

Juan and Jenni

My Angel Face . . . Siempre has sido rebelde y atrevido y quizás el más PARRANDERO de la familia . . . el más cabrón y el que en más problemas se ha metido . . . pero también eres el más FIEL y LEAL de nuestra familia . . . el más NOBLE de todos . . . y el cual ve y siente una gran admiración y un gran cariño por mí . . . gracias hermano . . . por tu sincero corazón y tus deseos de verme triunfar . . . por quererme y respetarme como lo haces . . . I'm here for you and I LOVE YOU WITH ALL OF MY HEART . . .
—Chay

Rosie and Jenni

Left to right (De izquierda a derecha):
Jenicka, Mikey, Jenni, Esteban, Johnny, Jacqie, Jaylah, and Chiquis

Sister, aren't you happy
we don't have another
sister? We'd leave her
out because she'd be ugly.
—Chay

Hermana, ¿no te alegra
no tener a otra hermana?
Seguro que la haríamos a
un lado por fea.
—Chay

Being a mother is by far my favorite and most important career.
—Momma

Ser madre es mi carrera favorita y la más importante. —Momma

15

Mikey and Momma

I finally understand for a woman it ain't easy tryin' to raise a man. You always was committed, a poor single mother on welfare, tell me how ya did it.

—"Dear Mama" by Tupac

@jennirivera 4 Dec 2012 "My favorite time of the day: la media hora en la cual llevo a mis hijos a la escuela . . . me fascinan sus pláticas y los pleitos entre ellos."

Jenicka, Mom, Johnny

La única que no me hizo llorar.

—Jenni Rivera

The only one who didn't make me cry.

—Jenni Rivera

@jennirivera 4 Dec 2012 "Paseando toda la tarde con mis hijos . . . ya rumbo a casa a descansar. Besos".

Family day at Disneyland: Esteban, Mikey, Mom, Jenicka, Kassey, Chiquis, Johnny
Un día en familia en Disneylandia: Esteban, Mikey, Mom, Jenicka, Kassey, Chiquis, Johnny

The girls prepped for *I Love Jenni* **on Mun2**
Las niñas listas para la grabación de **I Love Jenni** *en Mun2*

Jenicka's birthday
Cumpleaños de Jenicka

You are a good papa.
—*The Pursuit of Happyness*

Family Day

Día en familia

@jennirivera 16 Nov 2012
"While the world talks . . .
the Diva goes bra and panty
shopping. #lifegoeson ;-)"

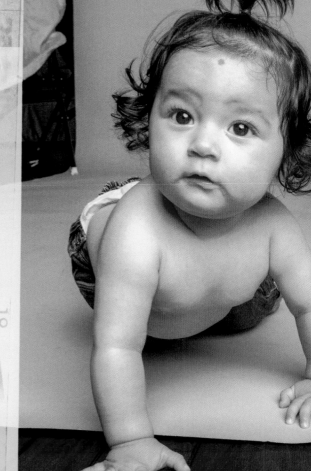

**Jaylah takes over
a photo shoot**
*Jaylah acapara la
sesión de fotos*

Jacqie, my job is to spoil her; your job is to discipline her.

—Wela Jenni

Jacqie, mi trabajo es mimarla;
el tuyo es disciplinarla.

—Wela Jenni

@jennirivera 17 Nov 2012 "Hace tres años nació mi nieta hermosa #Jaylah . . . Gracias a Dios por su existencia . . . se me puede caer el mundo encima . . . pero su sonrisa cambia todo para mí! Happy Birthday Jaylah".

21

Jenni in Her Words—
Simplemente Jenni

Diciembre "2006"
Abuelita hermosa querida
le deseo una muy feliz navidad.
La quiero mucho y le agradesco todas
su oraciones y tambien cuando me dice
"Chiquis la iglesia!" gracias, sin usted
esta familia estuviera perdida
completamente. La quenemos
mucho! Que Dios la bendiga!

Con amor y respeto,
Chiquis ♡
(Sunketa, la mas
grande)

Diciembre
24 2006.
Mi Querida Madre:
Muchas gracias mama por ser
tan fuerte y cariñosa, en esta navidad
le deseo muchas Bendiciones de amor
y le agradeseo infinitamente su amor a mi
y mi familia
Con ♡
su hija
Jenni

hOLA Abuelita
Te amo mucha
Feliz Navidad
Michael
Rivera

Abuelita!
I ♡ you
Y le deseo
lo mejor en
esta navidad.
tu eres la mejor
abuelita del
mundo !te
amo!
Jaqkea

22

December 24 2006

Grama I Love u
I wish you had
a merry Christmas

Janicka
Lopez

Muchisimas Felicidades Mama

En este dia tan especial
el cumpleaños de una Reyna
Que Dios me la cuide siempre.

Su hijo,

Happy Birthday, Mom

No matter how busy
or complicated
our lives may get...

...you'll always be
so very important
in my life
and in my heart.

Love Always

Para mi querida mi adorada madre y adorada madre La quiero con todo mi ♡! Jenny Rivera

Mom

Mi Querida y Adorada Madre.

Le Deseo todo el amor y todo lo Bonito. La Quiero tanto y le pido a mi Dios que me la Bendiga y me la cuide Sea feliz Madre. pase lo que pase, aprenda a ser Feliz La necesitamos

La adora su hija

Jenni

Que tengas un día
así de increíble,
porque San Valentín
fue hecho
¡para gente tan dulce
como tú!

02/14/08

Mi madre

Desde que tengo memoria
tú has estado junto a mí
para apoyarme
darme confianza
y ayudarme...

Desde que tengo memoria
tú has sido la persona
que siempre he respetado
tan fuerte
tan sensible
tan hermosa

Desde que tengo memoria
y todavía hoy
tú eres todo lo que una madre debe ser

Desde que tengo memoria
tú siempre has aportado estabilidad
en el seno de nuestra familia
con tus risas
tus lágrimas
y tu amor

12/4/08

Lo que soy hoy día
te lo debo a ti
y deseo que sepas
que te aprecio, te agradezco
y te quiero
más de lo que puedan expresar
mis palabras

~ Susan Polis Schutz

Mi Querida Madre,

Con todo el alma la adoro y le doy gracias a Dios por ud. Estoy muy poco a su lado, pero no dude en que le tengo todo el amor del mundo. Gracias madre por todo. Espero que tenga una linda y Bendecida Navidad con cariño

su hija Jenni

My Dearest Brother:

There really isn't much to say... except I really love you and missed you in the last month. I appreciate your being so true to me and promise to always do the same. I thank God you were born and cannot imagine my life without you.

Happy Birthday

Jenn

Hope your birthday brings you
the attention you deserve.

Hey, it's your day.
Do as you please.

Dear Brother

It's your Birthday (again)

So..... scratch your balls.

I love you dearly

Jenn

December 24
2008.

My dearest, most beloved brother.

It's been so long since I've written you.
Yet I've always had so much to say.
You know I'm really busy... so it's built up.
I want you to know that I love you just as much
if not more than when you were a baby in my arms.
I admire your soft heart, and respect your ability and courage
to change. I cherish your strength, and I need the lover
and respect you give me. Simply, I need you in my life.
Thank you for being around when we don't have anyone
else. I hope and know that 2009 will be your year.
Cherish it. I only want the best for you, brother.

Merry Christmas,

your sister
whom loves you,

Jenn

26

Feb 14 2011

My Beautiful Jackie
on this valentines day
and always, I love you
with all my heart. You are my Baby,
my daughter, my forever Valentine.
Please know that you can talk to
me about anything. My heart
is ready to listen and I
love you any which way.
But listen talk to God before deciding,
ask for his guidance in all.
You're doing very well Princess,
keep on going! Don't give up.
I'm very proud of you.
your momma loves you!

Momma

And I wanted
to make sure you knew.

Happy Valentine's Day

Momma loves you!

Momma

To My
Daughter,
with Love,
on the Important
Things in Life

Jackie

To My Daughter, with Love

June 1, 2005

A mother tries to provide her daughter with insight
into the important things in life
in order to make her life
as happy and fulfilling as possible

A mother tries to teach her daughter
to be good, always helpful to other people
to be fair, always treating others equally
to have a positive attitude at all times
to always make things right when they are wrong
to know herself well
to know what her talents are
to set goals for herself
to not be afraid of working too hard to reach her goals

A mother tries to teach her daughter
to have many interests to pursue
to laugh and have fun every day
to appreciate the beauty of nature
to enter into friendships with good people
to honor their friendships and always be a true friend
to appreciate the importance of the family
and to particularly respect and love our elder members
to use her intelligence at all times
to listen to her emotions
to adhere to her values

My lovely
Chunka:
Read this
and please understand what I am
trying to do
with you...
I love you
with all my
heart and I
need you to realize it.
Help me
Baby...

Momma

A mother tries to teach her daughter
to not be afraid to stick to her beliefs
to not follow the majority when the majority is wrong
to carefully plan a life for herself
to vigorously follow her chosen path
to enter into a relationship with someone worthy of herself
to love this person unconditionally with her body and mind
to share all that she has learned in life with this person

If I have provided you with an insight
into most of these things
then I have succeeded as a mother
in what I hoped to accomplish in raising you
If many of these things slipped by
while we were all so busy
I have a feeling that you know them anyway
One thing I am sure of, though
I have taught you to be proud of the fact
that you are a woman equal to all men and
I have loved you every second of your life
I have supported you at all times
and as a mother, as a person, and as a friend
I will always continue to cherish and love
everything about you
my beautiful daughter

— Susan Polis Schutz

Momma

Through Her Eyes—
A través de sus ojos

A court victory against sexual abuse

Victoria en la corte contra el abuso sexual

#Blessed

La pinche "pedsona".

—Wela

El hombre más importante
de nuestra vida: Daddy.
—Janney

The most important man
in our lives: Daddy.
—Janney

#JENNIsimo Arena Monterrey 2010

A birthday serenade

Una serenata de cumpleaños

Carnal the Pup gets a diaper because he doesn't know how to take a crap outside!
¡Carnal el perro necesita Pamper porque no sabe defecar afuera!

Birthday party

Fiesta de cumpleaños

@jennirivera 25 Nov 2012

"#yoconfieso que he andado de traviesa . . . jiji . . . :-/ pero ya regresé!!!".

#CartelDeLaDiva

Left to right (De izquierda a derecha): **Rosie, Jacqie, Chiquis, Jenni, and Jenicka**

In the elevator on her way to receive her place on the Las Vegas Walk of Stars
En el ascensor antes de recibir su Estrella en Las Vegas

After every storm appears a rainbow; this is Mother Nature's way of telling us to keep moving forward . . . This too shall pass.

El arco iris siempre aparece después de la tormenta; es así como la madre naturaleza nos dice que sigamos hacia adelante . . . Esto también pasará.

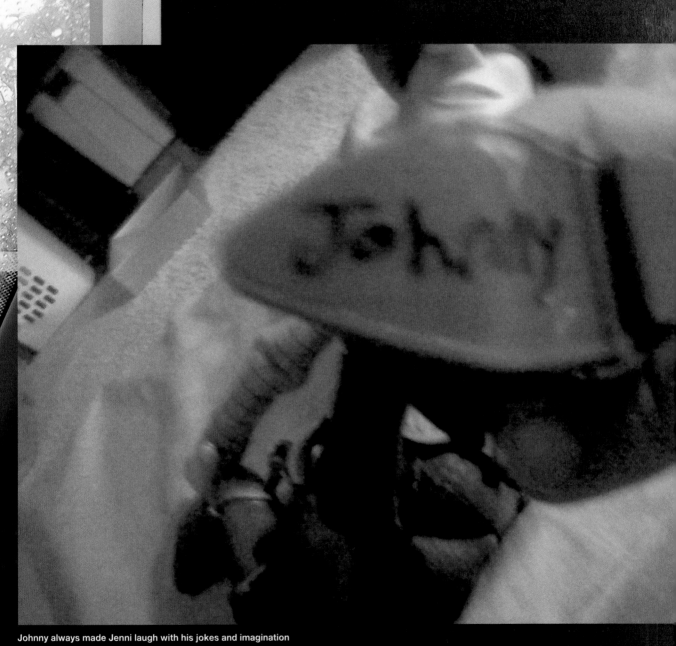

Johnny always made Jenni laugh with his jokes and imagination

Johnny siempre hacía reir a Jenni con sus chistes y su imaginación

Jaylah shopping

Jaylah de compras

#DivaTime

@jennirivera "I'm thinking about going on a diet, but I'm so damn delicious this way."

Jenicka and Jenni

Chiquis and Jenni

Mikey and Jenni

I can fly higher than an eagle, 'cause you are the wind beneath my wings.

—"Wind Beneath My Wings" by Bette Midler

Jenni and Johnny

Jenni and Jacqie

Husbands and the Love of Her Life— Sus esposos y el amor de su vida

@jennirivera "El idiota promete, el caballero sorprende . . . #DivaConsejo".

Chiquis y Trino en el primer cumpleaños de Chiquis
Chiquis, and Trino at Chiquis's first birthday

Inolvidable, así me dicen mis ex amores . . .
Tengo cariños que sí son mejores.
— "Inolvidable" de Espinoza Paz, cantada por Jenni Rivera

I will never forget what he said to me: "Forget singing. You're never going to amount to anything." This is the man I would wage battle against in the most important court case of my life. Even if it were to cost me my life, I wouldn't rest. For the love of my daughters. For my sister. For myself, as a proud woman. For my family's dignity and to use my voice to help other children who have suffered a similar kind of abuse. Life is something, isn't it? Look at me now.

—Jenni Rivera's address to the crowd before singing the song "Mírame (Look at Me)"

Nunca olvidaré sus palabras: "Déjate de la cantada, nunca vas a llegar a ser alguien". Con ese mismo hombre peleé en la corte el caso más importante de mi vida y aunque sé que me puede costar la vida, no descansaré . . . por el amor a mis hijas y a mi hermana, por mi orgullo de mujer y la dignidad de mi familia y para ayudar con mi voz a otros niños que han sufrido el mismo tipo de abuso . . . Lo que son las cosas . . . mírame . . . look at me now.

—Jenni Rivera hablando al público antes de cantar la canción "Mírame"

@jennirivera "¡¡Y esta es pa' que sepas cómo corre el agua, mijo!! Soy como el alka-seltzer, ¡¡¡el que me prueba repite, wey!!!".

Jen and Juan at Six Flags Magic Mountain. Jenni showed love and forgiveness when she sang to Juan, and she was by his side during the final days of his life. Moreover, Juan became her best friend. On stage, she dedicated the song to him "Qué me vas a dar si vuelvo (What Will You Give Me If I Return)."

Jen y Juan en Six Flags Magic Mountain. Jenni demostró amor y perdón al cantarle a Juan y estar a su lado en sus últimos días de vida. Más que esposo, Juan se convirtió en su mejor amigo. En los escenarios, Jenni le cantaba la canción "Qué me vas a dar si vuelvo".

During their marriage, Esteban gave her the most mature and peaceful relationship of her life. For the first time, Jenni felt that her family was complete. Onstage, Jenni would sing to him: "With HIM I live the way I never imagined, with HIM I feel what I hadn't before."

Durante el matrimonio, Esteban le dio la relación más madura y pacífica. Por primera vez, Jenni sentía que su familia estaba completa. En los escenarios, Jenni le cantaba: "Con ÉL vivo lo que nunca imaginé, con ÉL siento lo que antes no sentí."

Rivera-Loaiza wedding at Hummingbird Ranch, September 8, 2010

Boda Rivera-Loaiza en el rancho Hummingbird el 8 de septiembre de 2010

Wedding dress: worn once by mistake.

—Jenni Rivera

Mi vestido de bodas usado una sola vez, por error.

—Jenni Rivera

¡Ahora píquese solo, mijo!

—Jenni Rivera

@jennirivera 3 Dec 2012 "Ayyy PELÓN!!" . . .
"Lo de gritar 'PELÓN' en mis canciones viene desde hace
años . . . Mi tercer amor y por el que más me han visto
llorar mis hermanos . . . En un momento me pregunté:
'¿Por qué Dios me permitiría conocer al amor de mi vida
y no poder casarme con él?'. Meet Fernie, my soul mate.
Mi Pelón". Our song: "Is it raining at your house" by
Brad Paisley.

De gira con Fernando y Jacqie en Chicago, Illinois
On tour with Fernando and Jacqie in Chicago, Illinois

Jenni's Career— La carrera artística de Jenni

I'm nothing special. The "hood chick" that dared to sing corridos, "the *naca*" that decides to sing Mexican music. I'm also the "gangsta bitch" that sings in the rain.

—**Jenni Rivera**

No soy nada especial. Soy la muchacha del barrio que se atrevió a cantar corridos. La naca que decidió cantar música mexicana. También soy la "gangsta bitch" que canta bajo la lluvia.

—**Jenni Rivera**

47

The Beginning—
Los inicios de
su carrera

#JenniFact

I had no choice but to work hard. I was a straight-A student, graduated college, and I loved business. I never thought I was going to be a singer myself.

—Jenni Rivera

Mi única opción era trabajar duro. Fui una estudiante brillante, me gradué de la universidad y me encantan los negocios. Nunca me imaginé que iba a ser cantante.

—Jenni Rivera

I was the woman; I wasn't supposed to succeed.

—Jenni Rivera

Yo era la mujer, la que no estaba supuesta a alcanzar el éxito. —Jenni Rivera

Lupillo "el Toro del Corrido", Jenni "la Güera" Rivera, Juan Rivera "el Atizado", Gustavo Rivera "el Malquerido"

Rancho Farrallon: Brenda, Jenni, and Juan

It doesn't bother me that people think I'm too outspoken.
—Jenni Rivera

No me molesta que la gente piense que siempre digo lo que pienso.
—Jenni Rivera

Jenni singing to Lupillo on his birthday

Jenni cantándole a Lupillo en su cumpleaños

Jenni on the cover of a free magazine
Jenni en la cubierta de una revista gratis

Fernando Arau, from *Despierta América*, interviewing Jenni for the first time
Fernando Arau entrevistando a Jenni por primera vez en Despierta América

Jenni later went on to have her own talk show on Estrella TV and was in development of her own sitcom on ABC. #DivaWontBeMoved #Blessed

Jenni llegó a tener su propio show de entretenimiento en Estrella TV y estaba desarrollando su primer sit-com con la cadena ABC. #DivaWontBeMoved #Blessed

Quiero ser la Oprah Winfrey México-americana. Es una pequeña meta, ¿verdad? Eso es algo que yo quiero. Y no solo ser la anfitriona de un show, sino la dueña. Ese es mi futuro.

—Jenni Rivera #VoiceInMyHead

I want to be the Mexican American Oprah Winfrey. That's a small goal, isn't it? That's something that I want. And, of course, not just a host. I want to OWN it! So, that's in my future.

—Jenni Rivera #VoiceInMyHead

Her Team—
Su equipo de trabajo

Left to right (De izquiera a derecha): Julie, Jacob, Esteban, Jenni, Licenciado Mario Macias, Chícharo, Adrián "Vaquero."

These people met Jenni when she was the "new female artist who wasn't going to make it" and they stuck around by her side and got to see her reach the top and prove the world wrong . . . The Diva Camp, Her Team!

Estas fueron las personas que se quedaron con Jenni aun cuando se creía que era la nueva artista que jamás triunfaría, nunca la dejaron y le probaron al mundo cuán equivocados estaban . . . ¡El equipo de la Diva!

Jenni and Chavita. After separating from Esteban Loaiza, Jenni wanted to raffle off her wedding ring to raise money to help save Chavita, who was dying of cancer. But Loaiza's lawyers forbid it because the ring was contested in the divorce. Jenni was very sad and disappointed. Chava died a few months after Jenni.

Jenni y Chavita. Después de su separación con Esteban Loaiza, Jenni quiso rifar su anillo de bodas para salvarle la vida a Chavita, quien padecía de cáncer. Los abogados de Loaiza le prohibieron hacer la rifa del anillo, ya que era parte del divorcio. Jenni quedó muy triste y decepcionada. Chavita falleció unos meses después de Jenni.

Marco and Jenni

"La diva de las plumas . . . a mi publicista YAN-ALTÉ GALVÁN . . . gracias por tu pasión y dedicación a mi carrera . . . por verme crecer en esto que también es parte de tu vida. Por todo lo que haces . . . thank you!"
—Jenni Rivera

Yanalté, Jenni, and Juan in Chicago, Illinois

Left to right (De izquierda a derecha): Vaquero, Vero Nava, Chícharo, Elena, Esteban, Jenni, Zulema, Gabo, and Jacob
Not only her team, the friends that became her family!

No solo su equipo de trabajo, ¡eran sus amigos que se convirtieron en familia!

Arturo Rivera and Jenni

**Vanessa "the Hairdresser"
and Jenni**
*Vanessa "La Peinadora" y
Jenni*

19

18

59

8

To my CHIQUIS . . . my LIEUTENANT
in this DIVA ARMY . . . mija . . . you
have been my right hand . . . my
confidant . . . .my indestructible sol-
dier with HONORS . . . words can
never express how much I love you
and respect you.
—Momma

A mi Chiquis, mi teniente
en el ejército de la
Diva . . . Mija, tú has sid[...]
mi mano derecha . . . m[...]
confidente . . . mi soldad[...]
indestructible y con
honores. No existen
palabras para expresar
cuánto te amo y te
respeto.
—Momma

Angel, Jenni, and Julie

Jenni and Julie at an airport in Houston, Texas
Jenni y Julie en un aeropuerto de Houston, Texas

Many times Jenni's team lived moments with her that no one could ever imagine . . . from heartbreaks and disappointment to times of laughter and joy. Sold-out concerts at major venues to spending nights on airport floors. They carried her when she felt she couldn't go further . . . the reinforcement to her army.

Muchas veces el equipo de Jenni vivió con ella momentos inimaginables . . . desde penas y decepciones hasta momentos de risas y alegría. Desde vivir la emoción de haber agotado las taquillas hasta dormir en el piso de un aeropuerto. Ellos la sostenían cuando Jenni no podía más . . . eran el refuerzo de su ejército.

At Vanessa's baby shower, hosted by Jenni
En el baby shower de Vanessa, organizado por Jenni

Tere Flores: from cousin to assistant
Tere Flores: de prima a secre

63

Jenni, Vanessa, and Chiquis

Some of the Jenni Team are people that no one knows but are responsible for helping some of her biggest dreams come to life.

#JenniJeans #JenniSport

Team hug . . . Family ties. Jacobita, Jenni, Juliadora.

El equipo de los abrazos . . . los lazos de la familia. Jacobita, Jenni, Juliadora.

Muchos no conocen al equipo de Jenni. Ellos fueron los responsables de cumplir muchos de sus grandes sueños.

#JenniJeans #JenniSport

Fans

On this Thanksgiving Day, I thank God for you, my fans. For your applause, for your unconditional caring . . . for your support, which I treasure . . . for your prayers . . . for your love. Thank you for sticking with me in the good times and the bad. Thank you for being the (surrogate) parents who help support my children. I love you.

—Jenni Rivera

En este día de Acción de Gracias doy gracias a Dios por cada uno de ustedes, mi público. Sus aplausos, su cariño incondicional . . . su apoyo que tanto valoro . . . sus oraciones . . . su amor. Gracias por estar conmigo en las buenas y en las malas. Gracias por ser ustedes los padres que siempre han mantenido a mis hijos. I love you.

—Jenni Rivera

Torito and Jenni

I'm really in touch with my fans. Through their emails, letters, and stories is how I decide what music I'm going to perform.
—Jenni Rivera

I am just being myself. To me, that people are interested in Jenni, not necessarily the artist, but the woman . . . it amazes me still.
—Jenni Rivera

Solo soy yo misma. Para mí, que la gente esté interesada no necesariamente en Jenni la artista sino la mujer . . . aún me sorprende.
—Jenni Rivera

Marisela

Dayana

I will wait for you in heaven

En el cielo los espero

Alex

NOS vemos
este 7 en Colima
8- en Monterrey
I ♡ you!

Jenni & Artists/ Friends— Jenni y sus amigos

"Nadie nace sabiendo, ha sido un placer trabajar con y a un lado de ustedes. Gracias por inspirarme y darme la escuela que sólo la vida puede dar".

—Jenni

Canelo Álvarez

Elena Jimenéz, Vero Nava, Héctor Raphael,
Adán Terriquez, and Jacob Yebale

Gloria Trevi

Ricky Martin

Olga Tañón

Omar Germenos

Cynthia and Arturo Rivera

Cristian Castro

Ramón Ayala

Vicente Fernández

Joan Sebastian

Diana Reyes

Paulina Rubio

Carnalillo

Ricky Muñoz, Intocable

Jacob, Julie, and Juan

Diego Verdaguer

Valentín Elizalde

Faby Morales, twenty-plus-year friend and real estate colleague

Faby Morales, amiga de más de veinte años, colega de bienes raíces

Jeweler and best friend, Elena Jiménez

Joyera y mejor amiga, Elena Jiménez

Poncho Lizárraga, Banda el Recodo

Rogelio Martínez, Ninette Ríos, Arturo Rivera, and Jessica Maldonado

Signing the last contract renewal
at Universal
*Firmando la última renovación
del contrato en Universal*

Larry Hernández

Ser una cantante, vender álbumes, sobrevender los conciertos, tener un reality show, tener un rol en una película. Es increíble. Es maravilloso.
—Jenni Rivera

Being a recording artist, selling albums, selling out concerts, having a reality show, having a role in a film; it's incredible, it's wonderful.

—Jenni Rivera

Jenni's Legacy — El legado de Jenni

Giving Back—
Ayudando al prójimo

God gave me talent
and a microphone,
and He allowed me to
reach millions of fans
to make a positive
impact, a difference.

—Jenni Rivera

Dios me ha dado talento
y un micrófono, y me per-
mitió llegar hasta millones
de fans para hacer un
impacto positivo y una
diferencia.

—Jenni Rivera

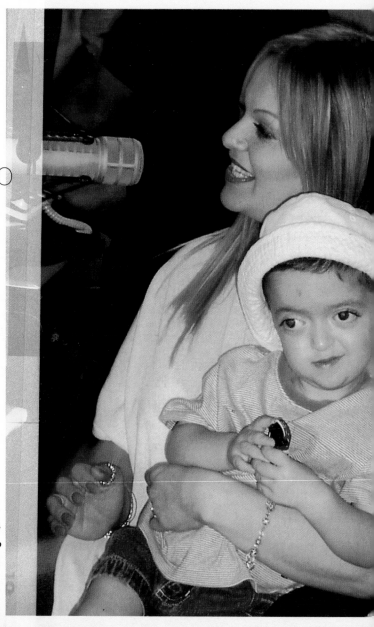

**The first child in need who Jenni helped.
She raffled off her favorite motorcycle to
raise money to save his life.**

*El primer niño necesitado que Jenni
ayudó. Ella rifó su moto favorita y así
recaudó fondos para salvar su vida.*

@jennirivera 14 Nov 2012 "RT @oghector: @jennirivera La meta es $3,500 ($1,500 cada uno) . . . so far, I have $1,730 raised. Faltan $1,770./// u got it baby . . . you'll have it this weekend".

This is what makes me happy.
—Jenni Rivera

Esto es lo que me hace feliz.
—Jenni Rivera

It is better to give, than to receive

Es mejor dar, que recibir

Hospital
LOS ANGELES
Children's
Televisa
Children's
ANGELES
at Kids Better

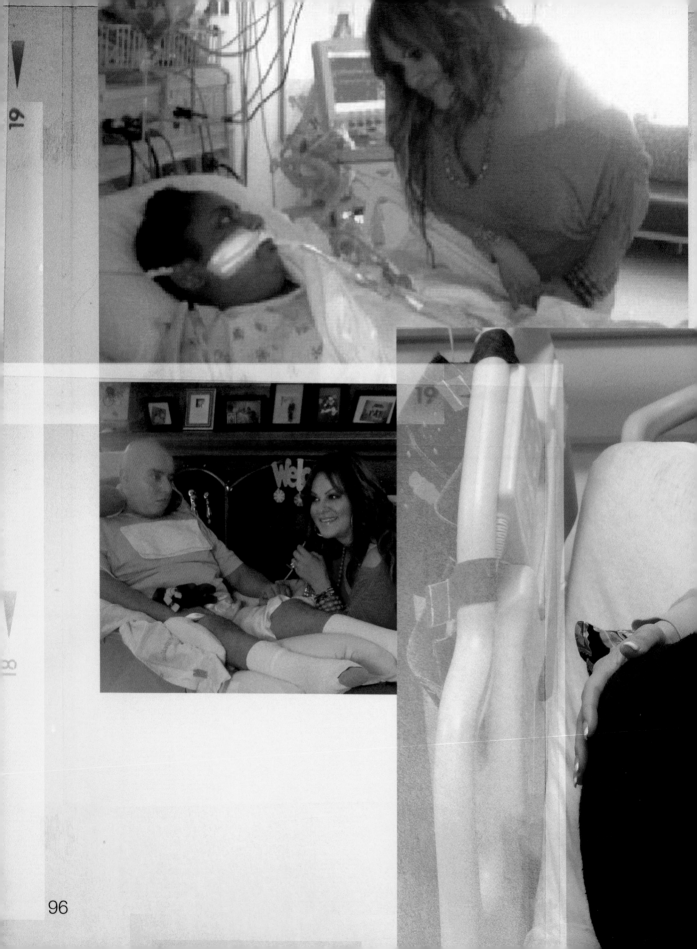

Freely give what you have freely received.

—Matthew 10:8

Dar por gracia lo que por
gracia has recibido.

—Mateo 10:8

98

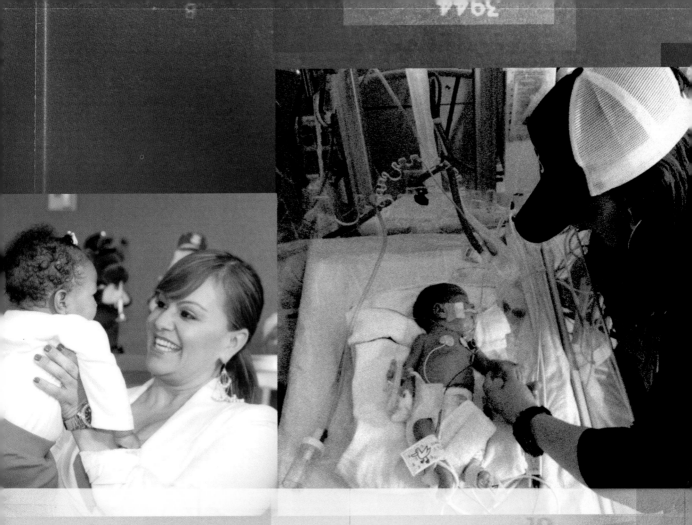

If you think you have problems, go visit a sick child in a hospital. Then you'll see your problem is nothing at all.

—Jenni Rivera

Si crees que tienes problemas, ve y visita a un niño enfermo en el hospital y verás que lo tuyo no es nada.

—Jenni Rivera

Jenni's Strength: God—
La fortaleza de Jenni: Dios

Pregunta para considerar: Ya que fui creado para vivir para siempre, ¿qué debería dejar de hacer, y qué debiera comenzar a hacer hoy?

frar más, hacer más obras buenas, ayudar a los necesitados — enfocarme más en lo espiritual — más tiempo en las cosas de Dios.

matthew 7

"For I know you, plans to not harm you, hope and a future Je

h 29:1

nothing's too hard for God

AG

CALL 1-800-4-PRAYER nothingstoohardforGod.org

@jennirivera

Pregunta para considerar: ¿Dónde puedo estar más consciente de la gloria de Dios en mi diario vivir?

sabiendo la verdad, sabiendo que todo es para el, de el, y por el. Para El es la gloria - haciendo/cumpliendo su proposito - Doy gloria a Dios.

Sabiduría - Entendimiento

8-22-08

Pregunta para considerar: ¿Cómo debería cambiar mi manera de vivir hoy, el hecho de que la vida en la tierra es sólo una asignación temporal?

08-20-08

dedicar más tiempo a lo eterno - a lo que sera mi vida cuando ya no este aqui. no aferrarme tanto a las cosas de este mundo que no duran para siempre.

"That is why I am suffering as I am.
Yet this is no cause for shame,
because I know whom I believed,
and am convinced that he is able
to guard what I have entrusted to
him until that day."

—2Tim 1:12 (*101 Faith notes, 101 God Notes*). #30

#DivaPrayer

Pregunta para considerar: Puesto que Dios sabe qué es lo mejor para mí, ¿en qué áreas de mi vida es que más necesito contiar en él?

1. confiar en Dios para lo que el tiene para mi futuro.

2. el me dara todo lo que necesito.

105

Adversity and loss can often become the rubber by which our life is steered to come closer to God. We re-prioritize and discover what really has importance, and what remains shallow and unworthy of our time and energies.

—*101 Faith Notes (101 God Notes)* **by Pauline Creeden**

1. Le pedire y le dire que quiero conocerlo mas - quiero que sea mi amigo

Dios no espera que seamos perfectos - solo 'completamente sinceros'

Dios nos escucha pacientemente

Dios tambien puede cambiar de opinion cuando le pedimos o sugerimos algo

el escucha nuestras quejas

Desear su amistad mas que nada -

Pregunta para considerar: ¿Cómo puedo no perder de vista la presencia de Dios, especialmente cuando lo sienta distante?

Dios dice: Nunca te dejare jamas de abandonare

9-19-08:
1. Orar sin cesar – all Day.
2. Say grace for our food.
3. No cuss words. CHANGE!
4. Be pleasant
5. Spend more time + give to the needy/church
6. Trust in God always!
7. Faith
8. God sees my heart.

I need to persevere in prayer. It's Major! It can help in solving problems tremendously, if not completely. God has the answer and solution . . . . I must persevere to wake up every morning before the sun comes out, to pray to spend time w/ him to know him better. Persevere In Prayer.

—Jenni Rivera, 2/18/11

Tengo que perseverar por medio de la oración. Es fundamental. La oración puede ayudar a resolver cualquier problema. Dios tiene la respuesta y la solución. Tengo que ser perseverante y levantarme cada mañana cuando sale el sol, a orar, a conocerlo mejor. Perseverar por medio de la oración.

—Jenni Rivera

cusing on ourselves will never reveal
ur life's purpose.

You were made by God and for God - and
ntil you understand that, like will never make
sense.

WHAT ON EARTH AM I HERE FOR?

t all starts with God. Ask him first ▽

August 7 2004:

I must be reminded that "he" is great
he' created everything and everyone.
therefore I am his creations — I should
think of that Constantly — and stop being
selfish — I am not here just for fun
or looks — but He put me here
for a reason — Realize it
Work it — Complete it.

3/19/09

ASK GOD –
whats my purpose?

I am not an accident.
God made me for a reason, purpose,
and mission.

god doesn't play DICE

We are the focus of God's love

To Be honest the driving force in my life is my work — keeping going on & not failing etc.

My driving force should be God, pleasing him, loving & giving to my kids & others.

I have a history of failing, making mistakes that cost me greatly in everyway. —
Yet, I believe God has a purpose — a mission for me.
I believe he can use me despite my mistakes, & defects.

I need to think about God's purpose and let that be my driving force.

I need more focus — motivation

it will simplify my life
it will give my life meaning.

I want to have answers for God and respond to him.

I want to please Him what He says matters or should matter

What will I say when he asks, "what did you do with what I gave you."??

I want to do what YOU want me to do Lord: Please — tell me — Show me what your purpose is.

REMEMBER, EACH OF US WILL STAND PERSONALLY BEFORE THE JUDGMENT SEAT OF GOD . . . YES, EACH OF US WILL HAVE TO GIVE A PERSONAL ACCOUNT TO GOD.
—Romans 14:10, 12 NLT

3/21/09

"Its" more than just here & now
we should worry and think about
God and what He wants
for us.

STOP · Cussing
procrastinating
Judging

Start · praying More.

I want ~~to do~~ things differently.
I need to in order ~~to~~ raise
my Kids better and ~~teach~~ them
~~the~~ better things.

Career:
Been there done that. I want
something "different" now.
As far as- purpose, meaning,
I want to accomplish more but
not at anyone else expense (ie: Kids)
I want to do More for my followers/fans

112

April 4, 2003. **Chapter 15**

Juan and I went to the Banda El Recodo concert at the Gibson amphitheatre. We had a good time ~~along~~ with Renan Almendariz Coello (El Cucuy), ~~and the memes~~ members of his crew and other staff of La Nueva 101.9 ~~For some reason I didn't wasn't working that weekend~~ Due to the easter festivities I had no gigs lined up for the weekend ~~so~~ we decided ~~to enjoy~~ go to the concert and hopefully have fun the next day at his friend Mike's wedding. ~~The~~ The concert was enjoyable. We sang, drank, and ~~spent some time~~ some quality time together. It was the last time we would do so.

~~On cope~~ The next morning I was to go shopping for something to wear to the wedding that ~~night~~.

"I'll give him thirty minutes to either call or come back home. If he doesn't, he will regret it." I ~~thou~~ He called back ~~at~~ 35 minutes later. I ~~let~~ past the time limit I had ~~sat~~. I got dressed and went out with ~~Erika whose best~~ my friend Erika, whose birthday had been the day before. We went to celebrate a ~~La~~ Mirage Night Club in Artesia. We had a blast. ~~I was determined to live a happy life.~~ It felt ~~great~~ beautiful to feel free for at least one night. No Juan. No problems. No arguments. Just Erika and I, the hip hop music, and my shots of Tequila. I was determined to be happy even if it was without my husband. I knew in my heart it was over. I knew exactly what ~~to~~ do to let him know I was serious. I spent the night at Erika's home in Anaheim. I didn't get home until 10:00 am the following morning. I had made myself cross the line.

everything matters

there is always / in everything an opportunity
to show someone something & love
      word
      growth opportunity

endure - while st tested.
pass the test → blessed → god promises a crown
of life.
    allow me to pass the test
    my lord.

what God has given me he wants me
to use faithfully and in the
correct way.

Because God owns it
I must take proper care of it

THOSE WHO ARE
TRUSTED WITH
SOMETHING VALUABLE
MUST SHOW THEY
ARE WORTHY OF THAT
TRUST.
—*Corinthians 4:2 NCV*

voice
knowledge
kids
public
my well being. etc.

114

God rewards us for using what he
trusts us with properly.

he gives us greater responsibilities
he promotes us.

I want a Good evaluation from God.

This world is not my home.
Don't get attached.

Life is a test, a trust, a
temporary assignment.—

God allow me to lose the grip of things
That are not yours or what you don't
want for me. P.S.

115

Wow!
God all my achievements,
prosperity, success and power
are not mine - It all yours.

Allow me to treat this life as
an assignment - I want & need
to serve faithfully. So that I
may receive my reward in eternity

Its in your hands

- My chiquis bonita
- products fragrance - clothing cosmetics merchandising
- Jackie - pregnancy relationship with her.
- Kids-
- Work career- opendoor if its his will
- new home.
  Bless Home.

I love your Word
thank you

things of this world are not what goina
last.

Father show me to rid of all that
is not good for me. Whatever obstructs
my view of you and what you hav

1. Trust Christ with your life —
he puts glory in me.

2. the more I focus on living for
God's glory. the more Joy he
give me — he fills me with Joy

3. Commit your life to Jesus —
one day you'll share God glory.

share god's glory in eternity.

Choose to Live for God →
Difficult. → Jesus give us
everything. we need to live for
god's glory.

I want to bring you glory!

God help me to be a better person a better example to others. I want to use God's gifts & trust to me in a better/more positive way.

Help me God.

Make me different.

God loves worship. It's a way to thank him - tell him how great he is.

The lord is pleased with those who worship him & trust his love.

psalm 147:11.

Worship - not spoken. its what we do with our life.

118

God gets pleased with worship
worship is a lifestyle.

I can work as if I did it for
Jesus - speak - smile - Be
polite - help others. give to
others.

Prayer

1) Spirituality
2) Dreznaos()
3) Kids - Teekia pregnancy - Chiques
   chun
4) relationship.
5) Businesses. fragrance etc
   Radio
6) Brothers / farm.
7) Direction on all the above.

Obedience → pleases God.
↓
proves we really love him.

God wants us to live for him -
for His pleasure.

Surrender → is what He wants -

Dying to self —

Jesus love us - we must
surrender to him -

protein shakes
eggwhites
veggies
salads
fruits
water
tuna
halibut
chicken breast
green tea

140 LBS

What do I want —

1) Move spiritually
   closer relationship w/ God → Pray more

2) Kids — Be closer   Morning
                                 Nights
   1 t: meals
   spend more time with them   w/ others

   time w/ me
   cook

THE HEART OF
WORSHIP IS
SURRENDER.

04/10/09

lox weight — 140 LBS —   1 hour cardio day
                         15 min — pushups
                                  abs
                            lunges/squats

121

Concerts — Los conciertos

Visiting Palenque offered Jenni a unique and extraordinary experience. It was the place where work stopped being work and became a celebration. Standing in the center of that arena was something unforgettable to Jenni. It formed a perfect circle of love, energy, and passion.

A Jenni, los palenques le ofrecieron una experiencia distinta y extraordinaria. Ese fue el lugar donde el trabajo muy seguido se convirtió en fiesta. Para ella, estar en el centro del ruedo era algo inolvidable, era donde se formaba un círculo perfecto, lleno de amor, energía y pasión.

Pues nos echamos un
PALENQUE

#JENNIsimo

During the darkest moments of her life, Jenni always found happiness on stage. The love of her fans soothed her soul infinitely. Thank you for bringing her joy.

En los momentos más oscuros de su vida, Jenni siempre encontró la felicidad en los escenarios. El amor de su público, una infinidad de veces fue el alivio de su alma. Gracias por hacerla feliz.

Even though there were rumors about an attempt on her life in Michoacan, Jenni always felt safe there. The fans in Morelia showed her all their love and support even after the Mexican army interrupted one of her shows. But Jenni wouldn't leave the stage. That's the day she uttered the famous phrase, "They pay me to sing, not to run."

Aunque unos años antes hubo un rumor sobre un atentado contra su persona en tierras michoacanas, Jenni siempre se sentía segura en todo Michoacán. En Morelia, su público le demostró todo su amor aun después de que el ejército mexicano hubiera interrumpido uno de sus eventos. Jenni se quedó firme en el escenario. Es aquí cuando nace el famoso dicho "A mí me pagan por cantar, no por correr".

#ThoughtIWuznt

The year 2011 was filled with highs and lows. After being criticized by some members of the press, Jenni feared her career might be in jeopardy. But after one of the most difficult moments in her career, more than 83,000 fans lined up to watch her perform at Querétaro. It was the largest crowd ever for a Jenni Rivera concert.

El año 2011 fue un año de altas y bajas. Después de ser atacada por algunos medios, Jenni sentía que su carrera podía estar en peligro. Luego de uno de los momentos más difíciles de su carrera, ochenta y tres mil fans pagaron por ir a verla en Querétaro. Fue un récord de audiencia en un concierto de Jenni Rivera.

#MariposaDeBarrio

FLR 1

FLOOR 1

AEG LIVE P

SAT SEP 03 2011 8:00P

STAPLES CENTER

JENNI RIVERA

2 6

Jenni was an enterprising performer, a risk-taker who did what no other entertainer in her genre had ever dared. She was the first-ever solo act at the Staples Center. Every seat was sold out and they even had to open up extra sections of the arena for the first time.

Jenni siempre fue una mujer emprendedora y de mucho valor, tomó el reto personal que ningún artista de su género había tomado. Fue la primera intérprete que actuó sola en el Staples Center. Se agotaron los boletos y hasta se abrieron áreas de la arena que jamás se habían abierto para ningún otro artista.

#1

Jenni's concerts were more than a job to her. She felt indebted to her fans and always gave it her all on stage. "I want you all to go home happy and feeling like it was worth your while to leave your homes to spend an evening with me." It's no wonder her concerts often lasted three or four hours. She couldn't say no when her audience chanted "Encore! Encore! Encore!"

Los conciertos de Jenni Rivera fueron mucho más que trabajo, Jenni se sentía comprometida con su público y siempre entregó todo en los escenarios, recalcando: "Quiero que se vayan contentos y que haya valido la pena que dejaran sus casas para estar conmigo esta noche". Por este motivo, sus presentaciones muy seguido sobrepasaban las tres o cuatro horas, pues siempre le fue difícil decir no a su público cuando gritaba "¡Otra! ¡Otra! ¡Otra!".

Gibson, September 8–9, 2012

After a successful concert at the Staples Center, Jenni decided to return to her favorite US venue. She felt at home at the Gibson Amphitheatre because the fans were so close to the stage. It was the last time she would set foot in her native Los Angeles, California. She would never make a concert set for March 2013, titled "Inquebrantable (Unbreakable)." Heaven needed her more.

Gibson, 8–9 de septiembre de 2012

Después del éxito rotundo que tuvo en el Staples, decidió regresar a su escenario preferido en Estados Unidos. En el Gibson Amphitheatre se sentía como en casa por la cercanía que tenía con su público. Fue la última vez que pisó un escenario en su tierra natal, en Los Ángeles, California. Quedó pendiente el concierto programado para marzo de 2013 titulado: "Inquebrantable". El cielo la necesitaba más.

#LaDivaSigueRifando

Culiacán is so beautiful!
In my next life, I want to
be born here in Culiacán,
Sinaloa. Cheers! I hope you
have a great time tonight,
that you leave satisfied, and
that you feel it was worth
your while to come out and
join me tonight.

—Jenni Rivera

Qué bonito es Culiacán; se me hace que en mi otra vida voy a venir a
nacer acá en Culiacán, Sinaloa, oiga, ¡salud! Espero que se diviertan
esta noche, que queden contentos, que valga la pena el haber salido de
sus casas para acompañarme esta noche.

—Jenni Rivera

Último Palenque, Culiacán, 2012

Last Palenque, Culiacán, 2012

#LaDivaDeLaBanda

God decided Jenni's last concert on earth would be in Monterrey. During one of the most difficult moments in her life, the Monterrey fans bid the "Butterfly of the Barrio" farewell on her journey to heaven. Jenni thanked them with the last smiles any fans would see. The night was such a success that she had planned a return engagement in February 2013.

Fue elegido por Dios que en Monterrey Jenni realizara su último concierto terrenal. En uno de los momentos más difíciles de su vida personal, el público regiomontano, con mucho amor a la Mariposa del Barrio, la despedía feliz a su vida celestial. Jenni les brindó sus últimas sonrisas. Gracias al éxito de esa noche, Jenni planeaba regresar a Monterrey en febrero de 2013.

And the tears come streaming down your face, when you lose something you can't replace . . . . Lights will guide you home.

— "Fix You" by Coldplay

We'll catch you on the flip side, Momma!

— Your Little Soldiers

¡Nos encontraremos en el otro lado, Momma!

— Tus soldaditos

Jenni with her kids at a restaurant

Jenni con sus hijos en un restaurante

You will be a crown of splendor in the Lord's hand, a royal diadem in the hand of your God. No longer will they call you Deserted, or name your land Desolate. But you will be called Hephzibah, and your land Beulah; for the LORD will take delight in you, and your land will be married.

—Isaiah 62:3–4 NTV

El Señor te sostendrá en su mano para que todos te vean como una corona espléndida en la mano de Dios. Nunca más te llamarán "La ciudad abandonada" ni "La tierra desolada". Tu nuevo nombre será "La ciudad del deleite de Dios" y "La esposa de Dios" porque el Señor te reclamará como su esposa.

—Isaías 62:3–4 NTV

Her children
rise and call her
BLESSED.

—Proverbs 31:28

Se levantan sus hijos y la llaman bienaventurada.

—Proverbios 31:28

About the Author—
Sobre la autora

Winner of fifteen gold, fifteen platinum, and five double platinum records, with more than fifteen million records sold in all, **Jenni Rivera** was one of her—or any—generation's most popular and in-demand artists, not only in Mexico, but also in the United States, selling out performances at such prestigious venues as the Staples Center, the Kodak Theatre, the Nokia Theatre, and the Gibson Amphitheatre. Jenni was also one of the decade's most award-winning artists. In 2009, she earned a record-breaking eleven Billboard Award nominations, becoming the first female regional Mexican performer to be honored with so many nominations. She passed away in 2012. On her forty-sixth birthday, Jenni's hometown, the City of Long Beach, honored her legacy by inaugurating Jenni Rivera Memorial Park.

Photo Credits — Créditos de fotos

Avalos, Fabiola, 56; Ávila, Vanessa, 64; Campos, Jacqie, 27, 45; Celia Hdz J1359, 142; Cruz, George, 123, 124, 128, 135, 136, 137; Galván Kent, Yanalté, 51, 52, 57; Hazelnut Photography, 12, 13, 15, 44, 107, 147; Hernández, José Antonio, 12, 21, 66, 129, 133; Lima, César, 53; Martínez, José Manuel, 68; Morán Jiménez, Sonia, 50; Muzel, Robson, 20–1, 89; Nava, Verónica, 76–7, 80, 82, 84, 130, 131; Quintana Pineda, Lino, 125, 126, 132, 134, 138–39; Rivera, Jenni, 16–9, 28–41; Rivera, Juan, 26; Rivera, Pedro, 3–9, 42, 48, 49, 50; Rivera, Rosa, 22–5, 52; ROYGTV MEDIA, 148–49 (Jenni Rivera's mural by Sergio Ramirez); Sánchez, Mónica, 140–41, 143; Sánchez, Vanessa, 59, 63; Sepúlveda, Héctor, 142; Courtesy of Universal Music Latin Entertainment, 88; Vásquez, Julie, 54–5, 62, 63, 65, 92–9, 101.

Special thanks to Jenni's fans — Alex Aguilar, Alejandra Avalos, Yaquelin Buenrostro, Manuel Chávez of Manny López Music, Dayana De Haro, Monica Flores, Juanita Guzmán, Betty Romo, and Noemi Valdiva — who shared their photographs of meeting Jenni with us.

All other images included courtesy of the Jenni Rivera Estate.